TEACHING STUDENTS
WITH
EMOTIONAL
DISTURBANCE

A PRACTICAL APPROACH TO SPECIAL EDUCATION FOR EVERY TEACHER

The Fundamentals of Special Education
A Practical Guide for Every Teacher

The Legal Foundations of Special Education
A Practical Guide for Every Teacher

Effective Assessment for Students With Special Needs
A Practical Guide for Every Teacher

Effective Instruction for Students With Special Needs
A Practical Guide for Every Teacher

Working With Families and Community Agencies to Support Students With Special Needs
A Practical Guide for Every Teacher

Public Policy, School Reform, and Special Education
A Practical Guide for Every Teacher

Teaching Students With Sensory Disabilities
A Practical Guide for Every Teacher

Teaching Students With Medical, Physical, and Multiple Disabilities
A Practical Guide for Every Teacher

Teaching Students With Learning Disabilities
A Practical Guide for Every Teacher

Teaching Students With Communication Disorders
A Practical Guide for Every Teacher

Teaching Students With Emotional Disturbance
A Practical Guide for Every Teacher

Teaching Students With Mental Retardation
A Practical Guide for Every Teacher

Teaching Students With Gifts and Talents
A Practical Guide for Every Teacher

TEACHING STUDENTS
WITH
EMOTIONAL
DISTURBANCE

A Practical Guide for Every Teacher

BOB ALGOZZINE
JIM YSSELDYKE

CORWIN PRESS
A SAGE Publications Company
Thousand Oaks, California

For information:

 Corwin Press
A Sage Publications Company
2455 Teller Road
Thousand Oaks, California 91320
www.corwinpress.com

Sage Publications Ltd.
1 Oliver's Yard
55 City Road
London EC1Y 1SP
United Kingdom

Sage Publications India Pvt. Ltd.
B-42, Panchsheel Enclave
Post Box 4109
New Delhi 110 017 India

Printed in the United States of America

Library of Congress Cataloging-in-Publication Data

Algozzine, Robert.
Teaching students with emotional disturbance: A practical guide for every teacher / Bob Algozzine and James E. Ysseldyke.
    p. cm.
Includes bibliographical references and index.
ISBN 1-4129-3951-8 (cloth) — ISBN 1-4129-3904-6 (pbk.)
    1. Mentally ill children—Education—United States. I. Ysseldyke, James E. II. Title.
LC4181.A37 2006
371.92—dc22

2006001773

This book is printed on acid-free paper.

06 07 08 09 10 9 8 7 6 5 4 3 2 1

Acquisitions Editor:	Kylee M. Liegl
Editorial Assistant:	Nadia Kashper
Production Editor:	Denise Santoyo
Copy Editor:	Karen E. Taylor
Typesetter:	C&M Digitals (P) Ltd.
Indexer:	Kathy Paparchontis
Cover Designer:	Michael Dubowe

Contents

About
A Practical Approach to Special Education for Every Teacher

S *pecial education* means specially designed instruction for students with unique learning needs. Students receive special education for many reasons. Students with disabilities such as mental retardation, hearing impairments (including deafness), speech or language impairments, visual impairments (including blindness), emotional disturbance, orthopedic impairments, autism, traumatic brain injury, other health impairments, or specific learning disabilities are entitled to special education services. Students who are gifted and talented also receive special education. Special education services are delivered in many settings, including regular classes, resource rooms, and separate classes. The 13 books of this collection will help you teach students with disabilities and those with gifts and talents. Each book focuses on a specific area of special education and can be used individually or in conjunction with all or some of the other books. Six of the books provide the background and content knowledge you need in order to work effectively with all students with unique learning needs:

Book 1: The Fundamentals of Special Education

Book 2: The Legal Foundations of Special Education

Book 3: Effective Assessment for Students With Special Needs

Book 4: Effective Instruction for Students With Special Needs

Book 5: Working With Families and Community Agencies to Support Students With Special Needs

Book 6: Public Policy, School Reform, and Special Education

Seven of the books focus on teaching specific groups of students who receive special education:

Book 7:   Teaching Students With Sensory Disabilities

Book 8:   Teaching Students With Medical, Physical, and Multiple Disabilities

Book 9:   Teaching Students With Learning Disabilities

Book 10: Teaching Students With Communication Disorders

Book 11: Teaching Students With Emotional Disturbance

Book 12: Teaching Students With Mental Retardation

Book 13: Teaching Students With Gifts and Talents

All of the books in *A Practical Approach to Special Education for Every Teacher* will help you to make a difference in the lives of all students, especially those with unique learning needs.

ACKNOWLEDGMENTS

The approach we take in *A Practical Approach to Special Education for Every Teacher* is an effort to change how professionals learn about special education. The 13 separate books are a result of prodding from our students and from professionals in the field to provide a set of materials that "cut to the chase" in teaching them about students with disabilities and about building the capacity of systems to meet those students' needs. Teachers told us that in their classes they always confront students with special learning needs and students their school district has assigned a label to (e.g., students with learning disabilities). Our students and the professionals we worked with wanted a very practical set of texts that gave them the necessary **information** *about* **the students** (e.g., federal definitions, student characteristics) and specific **information on** *what to do about* **the students** (assessment and teaching strategies, approaches that work). They also wanted the opportunity to purchase parts of textbooks, rather than entire texts, to learn what they needed.

The production of this collection would not have been possible without the support and assistance of many colleagues. Professionals associated with Corwin Press—Faye Zucker, Kylee Liegl, Robb Clouse—helped us work through the idea of introducing special education differently, and their support in helping us do it is deeply appreciated.

Faye Ysseldyke and Kate Algozzine, our children, and our grandchildren also deserve recognition. They have made the problems associated with the project very easy to diminish, deal with, or dismiss. Every day in every way, they enrich our lives and make us better. We are grateful for them.

About the Authors

Bob Algozzine, PhD, is Professor in the Department of Educational Leadership at the University of North Carolina at Charlotte and project codirector of the U.S. Department of Education–supported Behavior and Reading Improvement Center. With 25 years of research experience and extensive firsthand knowledge of teaching students classified as seriously emotionally disturbed (and other equally useless terms), Algozzine is a uniquely qualified staff developer, conference speaker, and teacher of behavior management and effective teaching courses.

As an active partner and collaborator with professionals in the Charlotte-Mecklenburg schools in North Carolina and as an editor of several journals focused on special education, Algozzine keeps his finger on the pulse of current special education practice. He has written more than 250 manuscripts on special education topics, authoring many popular books and textbooks on how to manage emotional and social behavior problems. Through *A Practical Approach to Special Education for Every Teacher,* Algozzine hopes to continue to help improve the lives of students with special needs—and the professionals who teach them.

Jim Ysseldyke, PhD, is Birkmaier Professor in the Department of Educational Psychology, director of the School Psychology Program, and director of the Center for Reading Research at the University of Minnesota. Widely requested as a staff developer and conference speaker, he brings more than 30 years of research and teaching experience to educational professionals around the globe.

As the former director of the federally funded National Center on Educational Outcomes, Ysseldyke conducted research and provided technical support that helped to boost the academic performance of students with disabilities and improve school assessment techniques nationally. Today he continues to work to improve the education of students with disabilities.

The author of more than 300 publications on special education and school psychology, Ysseldyke is best known for his textbooks on assessment, effective instruction, issues in special education, and other cutting-edge areas of education and school psychology. With *A Practical Approach to Special Education for Every Teacher,* he seeks to equip educators with practical knowledge and methods that will help them to better engage students in exploring—and meeting—all their potentials.

Self-Assessment 1

Before you begin this volume, check your knowledge of the content being covered. Choose the best answer for each of the following questions.

1. Emotional disturbance includes _____ of the population of students receiving special education.

   a. less than 2 percent

   b. about 8 to 9 percent

   c. between 10 and 20 percent

   d. more than 25 percent

2. Children who are labeled _____ are currently excluded from services under federal guidelines for providing services for emotional disturbance.

   a. schizophrenic

   b. psychotic

   c. socially maladjusted

   d. disruptive

3. During the past decade, the prevalence of students with emotional disturbance has

   a. mostly increased

   b. mostly decreased

   c. remained constant

   d. increased then decreased

4. The wide variation of prevalence for emotional disturbance between states results from

   a. having fewer students with the disability in rural than in urban areas

   b. differences in definition and classification practices

   c. some states having lower referral rates for special education services

   d. variation in student behavior from state to state

5. In most states, the prevalence of emotional disturbance is related to

   a. gender and age

   b. school discipline policies

   c. general age of parents

   d. intelligence level and social behavior

6. A condition characterized by loss of contact with reality, bizarre thought processes, and extremely inappropriate behavior is called

   a. social maladjustment

   b. schizophrenia

   c. social problems

   d. temper tantrums

7. Terms used to describe students with emotional disturbance may be similar to those used to describe students with learning disabilities and mental retardation, and most of the terms are

   a. educational

   b. positive

c. negative

d. psychological

8. Unproductive ways individuals respond in interactions with other people may be called

a. emotional problems

b. social problems

c. psychological problems

d. communication problems

9. Most students with emotional disturbance

a. have physical disabilities

b. have physical and mental disabilities

c. have mental disabilities

d. are physically like their peers

10. The primary area in which students with emotional disturbance are said to differ from their peers is in the area of

a. behavior

b. achievement

c. communication

d. learning

REFLECTION

After you answer the multiple-choice questions, think about how you would answer the following questions:

- What factors might affect the academic success of individuals with emotional disturbance?
- What factors might cause students to exhibit emotional and social problems?
- What do effective teachers do to provide support for students with emotional disturbance?

Introduction to Teaching Students With Emotional Disturbance

Mrs. Luanne Jones had been a second-grade teacher for 15 years. She had plenty of experience with students becoming angry when their needs were not met or when they were unable to do something; but teaching **Sandy** was different. Temper tantrums and sudden outbursts of anger that occurred when Sandy experienced frustration or failed to achieve a desired goal were a serious cause for concern in Mrs. Jones's class. Shouting obscenities, throwing things, screaming, crying, and trying to disrupt others were just a few of the ways Sandy would "throw a tantrum." Whatever form the tantrum took, it always interfered with productive interpersonal relationships and instruction.

Terry was a living legend at Magnolia Middle School. Everybody wondered what Terry would do next. Constantly asking questions, teasing other students, telling jokes, and generally disrupting the class were Terry's trademarks as a student.

Avoiding social interactions or failing to participate in social events was a way of life for **Bryce.** As is true for

(Continued)

(Continued)

> other isolated and withdrawn students, sometimes what Bryce did provoked rejection and exclusion by classmates and peers. Social isolation, shyness, or general social withdrawal interfered with productive interpersonal relationships, and Bryce was often depressed and unproductive in school; truancy and failing grades were becoming serious problems.

Students like Sandy, Terry, and Bryce are sometimes tough to teach because their behaviors interfere with productive interpersonal relationships. What they do violates expectations for what is accepted and causes concern for parents, teachers, and peers. For example, temper tantrums are common in very young students; but when they are part of the behavioral repertoire of older students and interfere with productive interpersonal relations, temper tantrums become serious behavior problems.

Disruptions are common during most school days. When one student is responsible for more than an expected or accepted number of disruptions, he or she may be considered to have a behavior problem. Similarly, when social withdrawal is occurring at an age when it is no longer considered appropriate and when it is adversely affecting school performance, it is a problem. Most teachers have at least one student with these kinds of behavior problems in their classrooms.

1

What Is Emotional Disturbance?

When students with behavior problems formally enter the special education system, they generally are labeled with one of several specific terms. The federal government refers to them as "students with emotional disturbance." This label entitles students to special education services, and the number of students identified has increased by almost 20 percent in recent years (U.S. Department of Education, 2000, 2001, 2002). States use various terms (e.g., students with emotional and behavioral disorders, students with behavior disorders). Although the states refer to this category in many ways, most use federal guidelines for **emotional disturbance** to formally define and identify it (Individuals With Disabilities Education Act, 1997):

> The term means a condition exhibiting one or more of the following characteristics over a long period of time and to a marked degree, which adversely affects educational performance:
>
> - An inability to learn which cannot be explained by intellectual, sensory, or health factors;
> - An inability to build or maintain satisfactory interpersonal relationships with peers and teachers;
> - Inappropriate types of behavior or feelings under normal circumstances;

- A general pervasive mood of unhappiness or depression; or
- A tendency to develop physical symptoms or fears associated with personal or school problems.

The term includes children who are schizophrenic. The term does not include children who are socially maladjusted, unless it is determined that they are emotionally disturbed.

Perhaps more than for any other category of special education, emotional disturbance has a definition that leaves much room for subjectivity and confusion. For example, there are no hard-and-fast rules or simple tests for deciding when problem behaviors constitute emotional disturbance. Consider the case of Susan, a fifteen-year-old who seems unhappy most of the time at school. Her classmates say she's in a "rotten mood" and avoid her. How do we judge the extent to which Susan's unhappiness is "general" and "pervasive" or normal? And what about Luis, a third-grader who does not get along well with his classmates or his teachers? Is he showing "an inability to build or maintain satisfactory interpersonal relationships," or is he within the range of so-called normal behavior?

There is much debate over the standards that are used to decide whether students are experiencing emotional disturbance. That debate focuses on the difficulty of measuring characteristics, moods, and abstractions (e.g., unhappiness) as well as on the definition's lack of specific behaviors that adversely affect educational performance. The debate is heightened by difficulties inherent in explaining inabilities to learn and build or maintain interpersonal relationships. Further, it is difficult to determine whether a student's behavior is caused by emotional disturbance or some other disability.

Students who exhibit severely aggressive behavior or who are extremely withdrawn are usually easy to identify, but most students who are classified with emotional disturbance do not display dramatic indicators. Sometimes, they are vulnerable to a particular teacher's tolerance for their behavior or a teacher's ability to redirect the behavior. Sometimes, students act "belligerent" or "uncooperative" because they simply do not understand English well enough to respond appropriately even though they may understand enough to get by in nonacademic activities and settings. In essence, to be labeled with emotional disturbance, a student must do something that bothers someone else (usually a parent or a teacher), then must be identified as "emotionally disturbed" (or, an equivalent term) by a sanctioned labeler (a physician, psychiatrist, psychologist, social worker, judge, or the police). These people try to be objective, but they differ in their perceptions of the seriousness and appropriateness of various behaviors; in their abilities to understand students of different cultural, ethnic, and social backgrounds; and in their views of how disruptive behaviors should be treated.

What You May See in Your Classroom

Students demonstrate many kinds of behavior problems. The magnitude of these behaviors also varies. We skimmed the professional literature to identify terms associated with behavior problems in school. They are listed in *Table 1.1*. Some of these terms are used to describe behaviors associated with learning disabilities, mental retardation, and other disabilities. Most of the terms are negative. If some of these terms come to mind when you think about a student in your classroom, you may want to take a closer look at that student's characteristics to decide if a formal educational assessment is needed. This assessment can determine if emotional disturbance is part of the problem and special education services are warranted. Your first step in helping these students is documenting the nature and extent of their behavior problems. Look for evidence of the following cognitive, academic, physical, behavioral, and communication characteristics.

Cognitive Characteristics

Many cognitive deficiencies are attributed to students with emotional disturbance. These students are said to have poor

Table 1.1   Terms Used in the Professional Literature to Describe Behavior Problems

aggressive	immature
aloof	impulsive
annoying	inattentive
anxious	irritable
attention seeking	jealous
avoidant	manic
compulsive	negative
daydreams	obsessive
depressed	passive
delinquent	preoccupied
destructive	restless
disruptive	rowdy
distractible	schizoid
disturbing	self-conscious
erratic	tense
frustrated	truant
short attention span	unmotivated
hostile	unsocialized
hyperactive	withdrawn

memory and short attention spans and to be preoccupied, overly active, and anxious, among other things. In general, students with emotional disturbance score slightly below average on intelligence tests, although the scores of individual students cover the entire range. There is no single cognitive characteristic that is a sure sign of emotional disturbance. Most professionals agree that absence of choice is an important consideration. For example, students with emotional disturbance may want to pay attention at school but may be unable to control their behavior to the degree necessary to stay focused.

Academic Characteristics

Most students with emotional disturbance do not do as well academically as we would expect based on their scores on intelligence tests. Students with emotional disturbance exhibit characteristics that *adversely affect educational performance.* This means they perform poorly on measures of school achievement. Students with learning disabilities also perform poorly in at least one area of school achievement. Sometimes, when students exhibit a significant disparity between the level at which they perform on intelligence tests and the level at which they perform on achievement tests, teachers question whether emotional disturbance or learning disabilities is the appropriate category under which to provide special education services.

Generally speaking, emotional problems can lead to academic problems, and academic problems can lead to emotional problems. When students are suffering emotionally, they can become very preoccupied and simply do not attend well to academics. Students who demonstrate behavior and emotional problems may be subjected to disciplinary actions (suspension and expulsion) that in turn limit their time in school and exposure to academics. And, when students do not perform well academically, their perceptions of their own self-worth suffer. They can become withdrawn or aggressive. Or a student's noncompliance may be labeled as "isolation" or "aggression" by a teacher who fails to understand that the behavior might be due to other factors, such as the student not being able to understand English as well as his or her classmates. Students who receive low grades may give up and begin acting out. Of course, other factors (including life stressors like parental divorce, a family move, loss of a parent or sibling) can lead students to experience both academic and emotional problems. In general, any signs of underachievement should be taken seriously in deciding whether behavior problems require further evaluation.

Physical Characteristics

Most students with emotional disturbance are physically like other students. The exceptions are those with psychosomatic complaints (in which the physical illness actually is brought on by or associated with the individual's emotional state). Students who have serious physical problems can develop behavior disorders, especially when a physical disorder leads others to act negatively toward a student, and the student develops an opinion of low self-worth. Physical complaints (e.g., stomachaches, headaches), absenteeism, truancy, and school phobia (i.e., aversion to going to school) often are characteristics you will observe in students experiencing emotional disturbance.

Behavioral Characteristics

Behavior is the primary area in which students with emotional disturbance are said to differ from others. The behavioral characteristics of emotional disturbance include an inability to learn, an inability to build or maintain satisfactory interpersonal relationships, inappropriate types of behavior or feelings, a general pervasive mood of unhappiness or depression, and a tendency to develop physical symptoms or fears. Many inappropriate types of behavior or feelings are said to be characteristic of emotional disturbance. In addition to the terms listed in *Table 1.1*, for example, students with emotional disturbance are said to be sluggish, fixated, verbally abusive, too orderly, too conforming, disorderly, self-injurious, isolated, irresponsible, disobedient, shy, secretive, bossy, dependent, psychotic, and noncompliant.

Some professionals have tried to organize the long list of behaviors said to characterize emotional disturbance by developing alternative classification systems (subtypes). For example, one system describes conduct disorders, personality disorders, mood disorders, learning problems, neuroses, and psychoses. Another divides students with emotional disturbance into those with emotional problems (those who internalize or keep problems to themselves and blame themselves for their difficulties) and those with social problems (those who externalize or take out their problems on others and on society). There is no accepted, right way to group these behaviors. We prefer a two-group system—emotional and social problems—because it is simple and makes sense relative to the concepts underlying the definition of emotional disturbance. Grouping behavior problems this way also provides direction for identifying appropriate instructional activities.

Bringing Learning to Life: How Bryce's Teachers Helped Him Improve Social Interactions

Working collaboratively with a special education teacher, Bryce's teachers decided to gather data on the extent of occurrences of the following behaviors reflective of general social withdrawal:

Sitting alone at lunch or another activity in which others are actively interacting

Failing to be selected by classmates as a team member or group participant

Failing or being rejected following attempts to socialize with classmates

Seldom volunteering answers or offering opinions during group discussions

Here's what they found for Bryce and a randomly selected classmate (in percentages that indicate how often each behavior occurred):

Behavior	Bryce	Shavon
Sitting alone	83%	35%
Peer selection	5%	65%
Peer rejection	75%	28%
Volunteering answers	3%	82%

Bryce's teachers decided that the social withdrawal they were seeing required intervention. Here are a few things they tried:

They provided a tape recorder and notebook for Bryce to use to communicate with teachers. This was helpful because it reduced the need for Bryce to have face-to-face conversations. When the level of Bryce's communicating increased, the teachers encouraged more traditional interactions.

(Continued)

(Continued)

They paired Bryce with two competent classmates for a "group spelling test" and set a rule that each member of the group had to spell at least one word on the test. They gradually increased the size of the group and the amount of interaction required of each member.

They arranged for Bryce to be in charge of key classroom materials (e.g., hall passes, headsets), so other students would be forced to interact with him to obtain them.

They kept track of improvements in Bryce's social interactions and frequently sent progress reports home (initially every day, then at least twice a week, then weekly).

Communication Characteristics

Although many students with emotional disturbance have language problems, there are no communication characteristics that are universal or specific to most emotional disturbances. Students with schizophrenia sometimes do demonstrate abnormal language and communication skills. Many never speak, while others develop language and speech disorders like echolalia (parrot-like imitation of speech), illogical or disorganized speech, and inadequate comprehension of verbal instructions. Students with schizophrenia represent a very small percentage of those classified as having emotional disturbance. Communication patterns for most students with emotional disturbance are similar to those of their peers; however, there may be some evidence of extremes in their use of language (e.g., more frequent lying, exaggeration, or overstatement; excessive storytelling; and intensive shyness during oral presentations).

WHAT ASSESSMENTS WILL TELL YOU

In nearly every state, students must be declared eligible before they can receive formal special education services. This usually means that a local educational agency team (that includes teachers, parents, and other professionals) conducts a formal educational assessment to determine whether the student has a disability and to determine that the student's individual needs justify special education services. Before conducting this evaluation, school personnel must obtain informed consent from the parent(s) or guardian(s) of the student. In making these decisions, the agency team must ensure that the disability is not due to a lack of instruction in reading or math or due to limited English proficiency. Further, the formal educational assessment to determine eligibility must use a variety of tools and strategies to gather relevant information, including information provided by the family and information reflecting the extent to which the student is involved in general curriculum. No single procedure can be used as the sole criterion for determining whether a student is eligible for special education services or for determining what constitutes an appropriate educational program. Teams are expected to use technically sound instruments that may assess the relative contribution of cognitive and behavioral factors, in addition to physical, academic, or other developmental factors. Another expectation is that tests and other formal evaluation materials will be selected and administered so as not to discriminate on a racial or cultural basis; will be provided and administered in the student's native language or other mode of communication; will be validated for the specific purpose for which they are used; will be administered by trained and knowledgeable personnel; and will be administered in accordance with any instructions provided by the producer of such tests. Functional behavioral assessment is one of the most widely used tools, providing relevant information that directly assists team members in determining the educational needs of students with behavior problems.

Functional Behavioral Assessment

Functional behavioral assessment uses a variety of techniques and strategies to diagnose the causes of problem behaviors and to identify likely interventions. This procedure goes beyond simply naming problems, focusing instead on identifying factors that start, maintain, and stop behaviors. The first step in conducting a functional behavioral assessment is to define the problem behavior in terms that are easy to understand and simple to measure and record. Effective behavioral definitions communicate what will be seen or observed when a problem is exhibited (e.g., Morgan makes irrelevant comments and inappropriate sounds during class discussions). Once the behavior has been defined, the next step is identifying contextual factors that control it. This information helps teachers and other professionals predict when a problem is likely to occur and provides a basis for deciding what to do to improve the behavior in the future. After collecting data on a student's behavior, and after developing predictions about the behavior, team members complete the functional behavioral assessment by developing intervention plans that emphasize the skills students need in order to behave in a more appropriate manner. Generally, plans that include teaching appropriate behavior and providing motivation to conform to required standards will be more effective than plans that simply serve to control behavior. The following section describes the strategies that teams may consider when developing **behavior intervention plans** for students with emotional disturbance.

2

What Should Every Teacher Know About Teaching Students With Emotional Problems?

S tudents with emotional disturbance receive special education because they have emotional and social problems that
require attention from teachers, parents, and other professionals
if these students are to be successful in school. Teachers who
are effective with these students know how to manage their
behaviors. **Emotional problems** stem from unproductive ways
of managing stress or activities (e.g., inappropriate types of
behaviors or feelings, tendency to develop physical symptoms
or fears). One student's response to having to wait for lunch
might be to become impatient while another's might be to
become very anxious. Anxiety, oppositional behavior, and temper tantrums are common emotional problems of students with
emotional disturbance. **Social problems** are the unproductive
ways that individuals respond in situations involving interactions with other people (e.g., inability to maintain satisfactory
interpersonal relationships). Disruptiveness, inattention, irrelevant actions, and task avoidance are common social problems of
students receiving special education for emotional disturbance.
Some general teaching tips for managing behavior problems are

Table 2.1   Top Ten Tips for Teachers of Students With
Emotional Disturbance

1. Establish rules for appropriate classroom behavior.

2. Establish consequences for inappropriate classroom behavior.

3. Praise students frequently for appropriate behavior.

4. Be consistent when using consequences for inappropriate behavior.

5. Teach appropriate behaviors, and practice them every day.

6. Use preferred activities as rewards for good behavior.

7. Monitor behavior, and post performance records.

8. Reward good behavior models.

9. Teach students to monitor their own behavior.

10. Consider developmental levels before making a referral for outside assistance.

provided in *Table 2.1*. In addition, you may want to share with family members the general information about emotional disturbance provided in Chapter 6.

Specific strategies for improving emotional problems are provided in the following sections:

Anxiety

Opposition and noncompliance

Temper tantrums

ANXIETY

A natural reaction to unknown or novel situations is apprehension or concern. A strong, unrealistic, and sometimes irrational fear is referred to as **anxiety**. Anxiety is a common characteristic of emotional disturbance. Being afraid of the consequences of actions, being worried about daily life experiences, complaining or displaying physical symptoms in response to school activities, and changing speech patterns (e.g., stuttering) are some of the ways in which anxiety is exhibited. The following strategies will help teachers to reduce the anxiety experienced by students with emotional disturbance.

1. To reduce anxiety, explore life events to understand stress. What events are stressful to students in elementary, intermediate, and high school? Knowing what bothers students can be the first step in dealing with stressful situations that affect their classroom performances. Commonly identified stressors for elementary school students include

Family problems such as parental disapproval, not spending enough time with parent(s), or adjusting to stepparents and remarriage situations;

Feeling different because of not having the same material things as others or not accepting themselves;

School-related problems such as a teacher not liking them, fear of failing, or failing to meet the expectations of their parents in regard to academic achievement;

School-related problems related to adjusting to different linguistic and cultural demands;

Discipline-related concerns such as being afraid of being punished or believing parents and teachers are too critical; and

General concerns such as being worried about simply doing something wrong or believing that something bad is going to happen.

Stressors for intermediate-grade students include

General adolescent concerns associated with adjusting to developmental changes, not having enough autonomy, not accepting oneself, or not understanding things in life;

Social problems related to adjusting to different linguistic and cultural demands;

Peer pressure associated with wanting to be accepted by friends, participating in activities (e.g., drugs, sex, and smoking), or doing things to feel comfortable;

Family problems related to dealing with stepparents or siblings or parents not understanding them, not feeling in control with others telling them what to do, lacking the resources to be independent, or feeling that no one is listening; and

School-related problems such as not doing well academically, not seeing the relevance of school, or not adjusting to different teachers, students, and academic demands.

Stressors for high school students include

Dealing with the future and making decisions related to accepting responsibilities, relationships, and the uncertainties of life;

Dealing with school-related problems such as getting good grades, taking courses to get into college, and teachers not understanding them;

Social problems trying to adjust to different linguistic and cultural demands or to deal with immigration at older ages;

Dealing with peer pressure and not being accepted, being afraid of doing and saying the wrong thing, and dealing with the use of cigarettes, drugs, and alcohol; and

Dealing with family problems like having different goals from those of parents, not having parental support, not having the understanding of parents, or having conflicts with stepparents.

2. To reduce anxiety, discuss and practice other responses. Have each student talk about something that makes him or her anxious. Have students role play ways to deal with each other's problems; then, have each student identify and practice ways to deal with her or his own problems. For students experiencing anxiety because of linguistic or cultural diversity, discuss differences that must be addressed when living in a different culture and have native language materials available for students to share with their peers.

3. To reduce anxiety, share anxious moments with parents. Find stories about children's fears and have parents read them at home as a special assignment. Ask parents to discuss ways to deal with the problem after they read the story; then, have the student go over these during a discussion in class.

4. To reduce anxiety, introduce new material gradually. For some students, being introduced to new materials can be anxiety provoking. Have these students engage in a preferred activity prior to being asked to do a new, less preferred one. Gradually introduce the new task while the student is still doing the more preferred one. Sometimes, requesting that only a small amount of the new task be completed can aid in "sneaking it" into the daily activities. Sometimes, introducing materials in a student's native language or letting students respond in their native languages reduces anxiety for students experiencing difficulties because of limited English language experience.

5. To reduce anxiety, share progress. When a student does engage in an activity that he or she was previously anxious about, make a big deal about it. Special awards can be prepared for such occasions and sent home.

6. To reduce anxiety, minimize the source of the problem. Initially, require that the student deal with the source of anxiety for only brief periods. If schoolwork is producing anxiety, require small units of easily completed work and gradually extend the level of knowledge and the amount of work required for completion. Tips for helping students with school phobia are presented in *Table 2.2.*

Table 2.2   Five Tips for Helping Students With School Phobia

1. Accept the student's fears, even though they may seem irrational.

2. Discuss the student's fears, and avoid arguing about them.

3. Have the student serve as assistant upon arriving at school.

4. Avoid allowing the student to return home once at school.

5. Make being at school especially rewarding.

Table 2.3   Top Ten Test-Taking Tips for Students With Emotional Disturbance

---

1. Be prepared (with pencil, eraser, pen, and paper as needed).

2. Review the entire test before answering any questions.

3. Estimate the time needed for each part of the test, and develop a plan for completing it.

4. Answer easy questions first.

5. Use an outline of key points when answering essay questions.

6. Try to answer all questions.

7. Identify your answers and write clearly.

8. Skip questions that are confusing and return to them later.

9. Trust first impressions, guesses, and responses.

10. Review the entire test before turning it in for credit.

---

7. To reduce anxiety, teach students how to handle their problems. Many students with emotional disturbance have limited positive experiences dealing with stress or anxiety. Often, they simply have not been taught how to handle these situations. Effective teachers address this problem directly. For example, if tests are producing anxiety, they teach students a few tips to make them better test takers (see *Table 2.3*).

OPPOSITION AND NONCOMPLIANCE

Students sometimes become angry when they can't do what they want to do or when their needs are not met. Others become physically or verbally aggressive when asked to do anything and simply refuse to do it. **Oppositional behavior** or **noncompliance** means not doing what has been requested by another person. Arguing, blaming others, crying, throwing things, breaking pencils, and tearing up papers are examples of oppositional behaviors. Tips for improving oppositional behavior and

Table 2.4   Top Ten Tips for Dealing With Opposition
and Noncompliance

1. Use direct requests rather than questions to achieve compliance (e.g., "I need you to start your work" is better than "Will you please start your work?").

2. Make the request while close to a student rather than from across the classroom.

3. Maintain eye contact when making requests.

4. Give a request only twice rather than several times.

5. Make requests in a soft but firm voice rather than a loud one.

6. Give students time to comply rather than expecting immediate responses.

7. Make more start requests ("Please start your work.") rather than stop requests ("Please stop whining about the assignment.").

8. Control negative emotions when making requests.

9. Make requests positive and descriptive rather than negative and ambiguous.

10. Reinforce compliance rather than ignore it.

noncompliance are presented in *Table 2.4*. In addition, try the following strategies:

1. To reduce oppositional behavior, ignore it. (Of course, this strategy should not be used if the problem behavior places the student or others in danger.) Pairing "planned ignoring" with attention when the student is not engaging in oppositional behavior is also effective.

2. To improve compliance, use lotteries. Each time a student engages in appropriate behavior (e.g., not whining when an assignment is made), place a small ticket with his or her name on it into a lottery box. Periodically pick a ticket from the box and provide a small reward for the winner.

3. To improve compliance, reward appropriate behavior in other students. Focus attention on students who quickly comply with requests and have them record their good behavior on charts that are prominently displayed in the classroom.

TEMPER TANTRUMS

Students with emotional disturbance are often frustrated by school activities. Temper tantrums are a severe form of oppositional behavior that relieves some of this frustration. Sometimes, when students believe the likelihood of success at a task is limited, they use tantrums as attention-seeking behaviors. Similarly, if key people (e.g., teachers and parents) are responsive only during or after a tantrum, the behavior may be reinforced and thereby continue. Try the following strategies to curtail tantrums.

1. To reduce tantrums, use cues to encourage alternative behaviors. Teach students with emotional disturbance to give you a signal prior to a tantrum. Set up a policy with your school administrator to allow the student to leave your classroom to "cool down." When the student becomes frustrated, have him or her simply ask to leave the room or take a walk around the school. If the student signals the need to express some anger, provide a means for it to occur at recess; throwing a ball against the school wall, jumping rope, or just talking through the problem can be useful substitutes for a tantrum.

2. To reduce tantrums, have a plan. *Reinforcement* is an event, object, or statement that results in an increase in the frequency of a behavior's occurrence. When the consequences of behavior result in increases in the behavior, these consequences are said to be reinforcing. Like any other behavior, if tantrums are reinforced, they will be repeated. Discuss with parents and other teachers the importance of developing and following a planned response to tantrum behaviors, one that does not reinforce tantrums. Encourage the student's parents to come up with a positive discipline plan in which tantrums result in withholding some favorite activity.

3. To reduce tantrums, let the class benefit from good behavior. Have parents keep a record of tantrums at home. Set up a criterion by which the entire class can benefit from the student's appropriate behavior at home. For example, once the baseline number of tantrums is obtained, an extra half-hour of recess for the class can be made contingent on a 5 percent reduction in tantrums at home.

Bringing Learning to Life: Tips From a School Psychologist Helped Mrs. Jones

Mrs. Jones asked the school psychologist in her school to help manage Sandy's temper tantrums. After observing in the classroom several times, Dr. Braitwaite made the following two suggestions:

- **Ignore some behaviors to reduce them.** If the temper tantrum does not place Sandy or others in physical or emotional danger, ignoring the tantrum may result in a decrease in tantrum frequency. This practice should generally be paired with attention when Sandy is not engaging in the tantrum behaviors.
- **Avoid rewarding tantrums.** Some of Sandy's tantrums are maintained by the attention received during or after the behavior. A time-out procedure can be a useful means of reducing the likelihood that the tantrum will be reinforced. This can be accomplished by placing Sandy in another room during the tantrum or by rewarding students who are not having a tantrum.

Mrs. Jones tried the suggestions. She ignored minor tantrums and paid more attention to Sandy when tantrums were not occurring. Mrs. Jones didn't have a time-out room, but used an alternative to control Sandy's tantrums.

(Continued)

(Continued)

She prepared a bulletin board with a card for each student tacked to it. On one side of the card, she wrote "in," and, on the other side, she wrote "out." When her students entered the room, Mrs. Jones had them punch "in" (i.e., turn the card to the "in" side), and, when they left, she had them punch "out." When Sandy (or any other student) was displaying inappropriate behavior (e.g., having a tantrum), Mrs. Jones punched the student "out" and rewarded those students who were punched "in." Sandy's tantrums decreased.

3

What Should Every Teacher Know About Teaching Students With Social Problems?

Specific strategies for addressing social problems are provided in the following sections:

Disruptiveness

Nonattention

Irrelevant activities

Task avoidance

DISRUPTIVENESS

Students with emotional disturbance often exhibit behaviors or actions that annoy or disturb others. This disruptiveness may be descriptive of physical and nonphysical behaviors. **Physical disruptions** involve body contact; they include fighting, hitting, pinching, and tripping others. **Nonphysical disruptions** include making noises, name-calling, making faces, laughing boisterously, talking loudly, and acting in a way that causes others to laugh during otherwise solemn occasions. The following strategies can decrease disruptive behavior in the classroom.

1. To reduce disruptiveness, keep track of disruptions. Clearly define the behavior that is disruptive. Place a small calendar chart on the disruptive student's desk, and inform the student that each occurrence of the behavior during a particular day will be recorded on the chart. No other consequence should be applied. Generally, this simple counting of occurrences will significantly reduce the number of them within two weeks. Students do not like records of their "bad behavior" kept as evidence that can be used against them.

2. To reduce disruptiveness, make being disruptive unpleasant. Making a student engage in a disruptive behavior beyond the point when the student has decided to stop can effectively reduce future occurrences of the behavior. It is particularly useful to arrange for the "extra practice" during an especially pleasant activity (e.g., recess) that the child must miss to do the "disruptive exercise."

3. To reduce disruptiveness, use group contingency plans to change behavior. The behavior of some students with emotional disturbance can be changed by two simple procedures. The first involves setting up teams within the classroom. Tell the students that occurrences of disruptive behavior (e.g., throwing objects, hitting others, shouting, whistling) will be noted during a certain time (e.g., reading period, before lunch, all day) and that the team with the fewest marks will earn a reward. Group members should be encouraged to support each other and to note periodically when a disruptive behavior is not occurring. An alternative group contingency plan can be established by having the most disruptive students be team captains and earn points for the team. The captain with the fewest disruptive marks earns a reward for each team member.

4. To reduce disruptiveness, speak softly to change some behaviors. Many students with emotional disturbance engage in disruptive behaviors to gain the attention of their teacher. When they are reprimanded for the misbehavior, the students often gain much desired public attention (e.g., class laughter) as well. By controlling the intensity of a reprimand so that only the target student can hear it, the attention-getting aspects of the disruptive behaviors may be reduced. When using this strategy, teachers find it helpful to comment also on appropriate, nondisruptive behaviors.

Bringing Learning to Life: Dealing With Disruptive Behavior

Many of Terry's behaviors were disruptive. Teachers decided to keep track of them to try to bring them under control. They used a small index card to note occurrences of Terry's disruptive behaviors; each teacher was responsible for a different disruptive behavior. One teacher wanted to decrease the number of times Terry called out answers during a class discussion. She kept a 3×5 index card in her pocket and made a mark on it whenever Terry blurted out an answer. Terry quickly became interested in these actions and questioned the teacher's behavior. Ms. Knozminor simply indicated that the actions were for the purpose of keeping track of something she was thinking about. The number of "blurt outs" reduced to zero within a week; the behaviors of several other children also improved when Ms. Knozminor was making notes.

NONATTENTION

Many school activities require sustained attention for successful completion. To do a math sheet requiring addition of single-digit numbers with sums under ten, a student must look at each item, compute the appropriate sum, and write the answers in appropriate locations. Not attending to any one of the components of the task will result in inadequate performance. **Nonattention** (distractibility) results when attention is drawn from the primary target to other more peripheral ones. Nonattention is a common social behavior problem that interferes with the interpersonal relations and school progress of students with emotional disturbance. Two strategies are particularly effective in decreasing nonattention:

1. **To improve attention, help students focus on what has been done.** Place small marks on written assignments (at the end of each line of work or after a specified number of problems) to help students see what they have done during independent work.

2. **To improve attention, reward appropriate behavior.** Before making an independent assignment, tell students that you will be stopping several times during the work period to reward those students who are attending to the task. Walk around the room while they are working and pass out "good behavior" tickets, or place a count on the chalkboard reflecting the number of students working when a "good behavior" check was taken.

IRRELEVANT ACTIVITIES

Engaging in productive or unproductive activities or actions not related to the task at hand is an example of **irrelevant activity**. Participation in irrelevant activities interferes with school progress because it limits the amount of time spent on relevant school tasks. The student engaging in irrelevant activities wants to clean the chalkboard erasers during a group discussion or use soap and water to clean the desk during independent seat work in math. Irrelevant activities are of concern when they interfere with the work of others. The following strategies will decrease the occurrence of irrelevant activities.

1. To reduce irrelevant activities, set limits on inappropriate behaviors. Acknowledge the importance of all the activities that students choose to do. Set up a system in which a specified number of irrelevant activities is permitted during any one day; this can be done by providing tickets that allow one occurrence of the activity and giving each student an individually determined number of the tickets. Behaviors that teachers permit to occur in this manner often become less important to the students, rapidly decreasing the rate of occurrence.

2. To reduce irrelevant activities, change your position to change behavior. The physical proximity of the teacher can have an impact on the extent and nature of a student's behavior. By moving closer to a student who is engaging in an irrelevant activity, a teacher can sometimes reduce the inappropriate behavior.

3. To reduce irrelevant activities, reward students for not exhibiting problem behaviors. Irrelevant activities, such as asking questions about inappropriate topics, can be reduced by providing reinforcement (a reward or recognition) when a student does not indulge in such activities during a particular time period. Initially, the time should be a brief interval; later, as the student reduces the level of inappropriate behavior, the time can be extended. For example, provide a token for each 30-second interval that a student does not ask an inappropriate question early in a learning sequence. Then, extend the time to five or ten minutes.

4. To reduce irrelevant activities, use differential reinforcement. Sometimes, problem behaviors that interfere with appropriate achievement-oriented behaviors (e.g., reading, writing, and so on) can be reduced by differential reinforcement techniques. By reinforcing predetermined low rates of some behaviors, teachers can keep these behaviors at levels at which they interfere less and thereby become more appropriate. By setting "talk-out," "bathroom request," or "pencil-sharpening" limits based on careful observations of a student's characteristic levels of each behavior, and then rewarding the student for keeping at or below the limits, teachers can help students reach an acceptable number of occurrences. Reminding the student each hour that targeted behavior is within the expected limits will help to make the initial trials more likely to succeed.

TASK AVOIDANCE

A common way of handling tasks that are not particularly interesting or appealing is to postpone the task or elaborately prepare for it. This type of behavior is sometimes referred to as **task**

avoidance or procrastination; think of the term papers you could have written while you were getting ready to write one. Opportunities for task avoidance include a variety of behaviors related to beginning the task, actually working at the task, and completing the task. Task avoidance is a problem only when it results in individual nonproductivity or when it negatively influences the productivity of others. The classic example of task avoidance is demonstrated by the student who asks permission to sharpen a pencil so many times that the pencil is reduced to a worthless stub, and the student then complains: "I can't do the work because I don't have a pencil." Reducing task avoidance can be accomplished by implementing the following strategies.

1. To reduce task avoidance, break large assignments into smaller units. If an assignment is particularly long or unusually tedious, it is helpful to break it up into smaller units and to divide the work time into different types of sessions. Some students with emotional disturbance like working on a tough assignment for 15–20 minutes (sometimes less) and then taking a short break before completing the next portion.

2. To reduce task avoidance, increase the payoff for doing work. Prepare a series of reading passages that include important messages within them. For example, after several paragraphs, insert into the text a sentence such as "After you read this, come to my desk for a reward" or "After you read this, bring a pencil to my desk for a reward." After several students have "found the treasure," point out to the others (especially the task-avoiding student) what happened. Let the student know that the same activity will be used again in the future, but don't provide rewards once the "secret" is out.

3. To reduce task avoidance, develop many plans for task completion. Students with emotional disturbance who have problems involving task avoidance often are not effective work planners; they seldom develop a plan before doing an assignment and almost never use one while doing their work. The value of plans can be illustrated by using homework as a target task. First, identify several comparable assignments for this activity. Next, with the student, plan several completion strategies for getting the work done after school. For example, using blocks of time (e.g., 4:00–5:00, 5:00–6:00, 6:00–7:00), develop at least three plans for when work, play, and other activities will be done. Have the student select one plan for use on the first day of the activity; contact parents to alert them to the plan. Have the student record the amount of time the assignment required and his or her accuracy. Repeat the procedure using a different plan each day and compare the effectiveness of the plans.

4

What Trends and Issues Influence How We Teach Students With Emotional Disturbance?

The contention that schools are not identifying students with emotional disturbance is generating considerable discussion today. The concern is that students with behavior problems requiring special attention are not receiving services needed to bring about the changes necessary for their success in school. This controversy has given some states the impetus to develop definitions that are more relevant educationally, to formalize and improve systematic procedures for identification, and to encourage alternative service delivery models (among them, school-based mental health services).

AN EVOLVING DEFINITION

In recent amendments of the Individuals With Disabilities Education Act (1997), "seriously" was removed from the language used to define and describe students with emotional disturbance; the terminology for this disability now reads "emotionally disturbed" rather than "seriously emotionally disturbed." The currently accepted definition for "emotionally disturbed" excludes students who are socially maladjusted. Some argue that this is a good idea, and others say it leads to underidentification and is just a way to cut costs. Excluding social maladjustment in the definition has also caused professional debate, largely because of the lack of a generally accepted definition of social maladjustment (Coleman & Webber, 2002; Council for Children With Behavioral Disorders, 1987). It is as if professionals agreed to define mental retardation as significantly subaverage general intelligence without having an accepted standard for intelligence. And, the problem is further complicated by the absence of any evidence justifying the decision to separate social maladjustment (delinquency and social deviance) from emotional disturbance (emotional and social problems). In some states, professionals are rethinking the definition of emotional disturbance to better address these concerns.

A common concern in special education is the appropriateness of the terminology and definitions used as guidelines for groups of students. Emotional disturbance is the most recent category to experience definitional debate. As this module was going to press, a new substitute terminology and definition for this group of students was proposed and being seriously discussed by professionals in special education and mental health services. Congress directed the U.S. Secretary of Education to issue a "Notice of Inquiry" soliciting public and professional opinion on

1. The need to revise the current definition of emotional disturbance.

2. Whether the term "emotional and behavioral disorders" and its related definition [which follows] should be used in its place.

> The term "emotional and behavioral disorder" means a disability that is—
> (i) characterized by behavioral or emotional responses in school programs so different from appropriate age, cultural, or ethnic norms that they adversely affect educational performance (academic, social, vocational, and personal skills);

(ii) more than a temporary, expected response to stressful events in the environment;

(iii) consistently exhibited in two different settings, at least one of which is school-related, and

(iv) unresponsive to direct intervention applied in general education, or the condition of the child is such that general education interventions would be insufficient.

The term includes such a disability that co-exists with other disabilities.

The term includes a schizophrenic disorder, affective disorder, anxiety disorder, or other sustained disorder of conduct or adjustment, affecting a child, if the disorder affects educational performance as described earlier.

As has been the case with other categories, the need for action is justified by inadequacies in past practices and the anticipated benefits of change. For example, problems with the current definition include the fact that five criteria are not supported by previous or current research, that adverse educational performance is often narrowly interpreted to mean only academics, that it is the only category with the "severity" modifier, and that it excludes "social maladjustment." The virtue of the new terminology and definition is that both are delimited (e.g., they reference age, cultural, and ethnic norms; include key academic skills areas and widely recognized problems of mental health; and require evidence from multiple settings to control biased decision making). When all is said and done, the goal of special education is improved, and students with disabilities are better served by improved definitions and terminology.

MEDICAL TREATMENT

The use of medication in the treatment of behavior problems is widespread. Stimulants, minor tranquilizers, and major tranquilizers are commonly used with students with emotional disturbance. The goal in prescribing drugs is to control behavior, but, too often, the side effects outweigh the advantages.

Additionally, students sometimes develop drug dependencies that are not physically or emotionally healthy. Of course, teachers and school personnel do not prescribe medications. Physicians prescribe them and rely on parents, teachers, and school personnel to monitor the effects. No single factor can be blamed if medication is abused in the treatment of students. The probability is very high that if you teach, you will have a student who is on medication. The best thing to remember is that monitoring helps physicians and parents decide whether a medication is working and whether its effects are beneficial or detrimental.

5

*Emotional Disturbance
in Perspective*

I f you ask teachers what group of students they least prefer
to have in their classrooms, they will probably say those with
behavior problems. Discipline and classroom management consistently are ranked among the most serious problems and areas
of greatest need in surveys of public and professional opinions
about education (Rose & Gallup, 2002, 2003, 2004). This need
continues to be felt despite the fact that teacher preparation programs provide considerable information about how to handle
discipline problems.

Arguments about the definition of emotional disturbance
continue despite evidence that teachers need help meeting
the social and emotional needs of students exhibiting problem
behaviors in school. This troubles us. Time spent arguing about
definitions is bound by a law of diminishing returns. There will
never be a perfect definition for any category of special education. All definitions that currently exist, and all before them, can
be (and most have been) criticized as too exclusive, too inclusive,
too inadequate, too conservative, or too liberal to be useful to all
people. This is just the way it is. While a definition drives practice, laboring over the definition should not become practice.
Special education is an area of successive approximations. As
long as people know whom the category is intended to include,

the definition is adequate (not perfect, not without flaw, not useless, just adequate). The more important job of deciding how to help students who meet the implied criteria or stated definition should take center stage.

The boundaries between categories are fuzzy. Differences between the emotional disturbance category and that of learning disabilities or mental retardation or social maladjustment are not like those between the categories describing sensory disabilities, such as deafness and blindness. Emotional disturbance is the most subjective special education category. Judgment is a key factor.

Typically, teachers, school psychologists, and counselors gather data over a relatively long time before deciding whether emotional disturbance is an appropriate category for a student experiencing problems in school. Often, professionals from mental health and social service agencies are also involved in the identification and treatment of these students. Teachers are expected to work closely with outside agency personnel to supply information during identification and intervention activities. But sometimes this information is limited by factors such as when it is collected, where it is collected, and who collects it. Behaviors judged normal at one time in one educational or community setting might be judged abnormal at another time, in another setting, or by a different person. And, although they may disagree about the extent to which certain behaviors are representative of emotional disturbance, classroom teachers do agree on one thing: Students who disrupt classes are not among their favorites. Regardless, these students are entitled to education, and we believe it should be provided in classrooms with their neighbors and peers. This means providing teachers with support—a goal that can and should be achieved. Clearly, emotional disturbance is a category about which the adage, "it's all in how you look at it" is appropriate.

An existential philosopher might ask, "If a tree falls in the forest and nobody hears it, does it make a sound?" An existential professional in the area of emotional disturbance might ask, "If a student exhibits a behavior and nobody is bothered by it, is it a problem?" From this perspective, emotional disturbance and behavior problems are "in the eye of the beholder." "It's all in how you look at it," then, makes sense as a philosophy for teaching these students. For example, teachers provided the following illustrations that reflect their experiences with students with emotional disturbance (Anderegg et al., 1993):

Most Unforgettable Characters

The student who could lose his pencil while writing with it.

The child who conversed with light bulbs.

The kid who still fought while in a body cast.

Most Embarrassing Moments in the Classroom

"Hey Teach, I can see your bikini panty line."

Needing to borrow lunch money from my students.

Saying 'no' to former student visiting from prison.

Favorite Daydreams of Teachers of Students With [Emotional Disturbance]

Sensory deprivation therapy.

Instruments of torture.

Giving directions once and having everybody follow them.

Watching an administrator teach my class for a day.

Lunch without kids.

Indecent proposals . . . from an adult. (pp. 24–25)

While the content and tone here are intended to be humorous and comforting, the message we want to leave you with is that students with emotional disturbance (or any other disability) are people with dreams, desires, disappointments, and deeds like everybody else. And, while many find these students the most difficult to teach, many others find their antics interesting, exciting, and acceptable beginnings for the process of change that is part of any education. Some see the glass as half empty, and some see it as half full. In special education, especially when dealing with students with emotional disturbance, it's all in how you look at it.

6

What Have We Learned?

As you complete your study of teaching students with emotional disturbance, it may be helpful to review what you have learned. To help you check your understanding, we have listed the key points and key vocabulary for you to review. We have included the Self-Assessment again, so you can compare what you know now with what you knew as you began your study. Finally, we provide a few topics for you to think about and some activities for you to do "on your own."

KEY POINTS

▣ Emotional disturbance is reflected in inappropriate behaviors that adversely affect educational performance.

▣ Although specific emotional and social behaviors are not included in accepted definitions for this category, most professionals agree that students' educational performances are adversely affected by how they personally handle stress and challenges (emotional problems) and how they interact in other situations (social problems).

▣ Emotional problems of students with emotional disturbance include anxiety, temper tantrums, and low self-concept.

◙ Specific social problems include disruptiveness, nonattention, irrelevant activities, and task avoidance.

◙ Interventions for students with emotional disturbance generally focus on identifying stressors, rewarding appropriate behavior, discouraging inappropriate behaviors, and coordinating school efforts with efforts in the home and community.

More About Emotional Disturbance in the Classroom

National Dissemination Center for Children With Disabilities (NICHCY) Fact Sheet 5: Emotional Disturbance

Incidence

In the 2000–2001 school year, 473,663 children and youth with an emotional disturbance were provided special education and related services in the public schools (*Twenty-fourth Annual Report to Congress*, U.S. Department of Education, 2002).

Characteristics

The causes of emotional disturbance have not been adequately determined. Although various factors such as heredity, brain disorder, diet, stress, and family functioning have been suggested as possible causes, research has not shown any of these factors to be the direct cause of behavior or emotional problems. Some of the characteristics and behaviors seen in children who have emotional disturbances include:

- Hyperactivity (short attention span, impulsiveness);
- Aggression/self-injurious behavior (acting out, fighting);
- Withdrawal (failure to initiate interaction with others; retreat from exchanges of social interaction, excessive fear or anxiety);

- Immaturity (inappropriate crying, temper tantrums, poor coping skills); and
- Learning difficulties (academically performing below grade level).

Children with the most serious emotional disturbances may exhibit distorted thinking, excessive anxiety, bizarre motor acts, and abnormal mood swings. Some are identified as children who have a severe psychosis or schizophrenia.

Many children who do not have emotional disturbances may display some of these same behaviors at various times during their development. However, when children have an emotional disturbance, these behaviors continue over long periods of time. Their behavior thus signals that they are not coping with their environment or peers.

Educational Implications

The educational programs for children with an emotional disturbance need to include attention to providing emotional and behavioral support as well as helping them to master academics, develop social skills, and increase self-awareness, self-control, and self-esteem. A large body of research exists regarding methods of providing students with positive behavioral support (PBS) in the school environment, so that problem behaviors are minimized and positive, appropriate behaviors are fostered. . . . It is also important to know that, within the school setting:

- For a child whose behavior impedes learning (including the learning of others), the team developing the child's Individualized Education Program (IEP) needs to consider, if appropriate, strategies to address that behavior, including positive behavioral interventions, strategies, and supports.

(Continued)

(Continued)

- Students eligible for special education services under the category of emotional disturbance may have IEPs that include psychological or counseling services. These are important related services which are available under law and are to be provided by a qualified social worker, psychologist, guidance counselor, or other qualified personnel.
- Career education (both vocational and academic) is also a major part of secondary education and should be a part of the transition plan included in every adolescent's IEP.

There is growing recognition that families, as well as their children, need support, respite care, intensive case management, and a collaborative, multi-agency approach to services. Many communities are working toward providing these wrap-around services. There are a growing number of agencies and organizations actively involved in establishing support services in the community.

Other Considerations

Families of children with emotional disturbances may need help in understanding their children's condition and in learning how to work effectively with them. Help is available from psychiatrists, psychologists, or other mental health professionals in public or private mental health settings. Children should be provided services based on their individual needs, and all persons who are involved with these children should be aware of the care they are receiving. It is important to coordinate all services between home, school, and therapeutic community with open communication.

Source: Used with the permission of the National Dissemination Center for Children with Disabilities (2005).

KEY VOCABULARY

Anxiety is a strong, unrealistic, and sometimes irrational fear.

Behavior intervention plans describe strategies that teams may consider when providing services for students with emotional disturbance.

Distractibility (nonattention) results when attention is drawn from the primary target to other more peripheral ones.

Emotional problems stem from unproductive ways of managing stress or activities (e.g., inappropriate types of behaviors or feelings or the tendency to develop physical symptoms or fears).

Functional behavioral assessment uses a variety of techniques and strategies to diagnose the causes of problem behaviors and to identify likely interventions.

Irrelevant activity means engaging in productive or unproductive activities or actions not related to the task at hand.

Nonattention (distractibility) results when attention is drawn from the primary target to other more peripheral ones.

Noncompliance or oppositional behavior means not doing what has been requested by another person.

Nonphysical disruptions include making noises, name-calling, making faces, laughing boisterously, talking loudly, and acting in a way that causes others to laugh during otherwise solemn occasions.

Oppositional behavior or noncompliance means not doing what has been requested by another person.

Physical disruptions involve body contact; they include fighting, hitting, pinching, and tripping others.

Social problems are unproductive ways in which individuals respond in situations involving interactions with other people (e.g., inability to maintain satisfactory interpersonal relationships).

Task avoidance or procrastination is a common way of handling tasks that are not particularly interesting or appealing by postponing attention to the task or elaborately preparing for it.

Temper tantrums are a severe form of oppositional behavior.

Self-Assessment 2

A fter you complete this book, check your knowledge and understanding of the content covered. Choose the best answer for each of the following questions.

1. Emotional disturbance includes _____ of the population of students receiving special education.

    a. less than 2 percent

    b. about 8 to 9 percent

    c. between 10 and 20 percent

    d. more than 25 percent

2. Children who are labeled _____ are currently excluded from services under federal guidelines for providing services for emotional disturbance.

    a. schizophrenic

    b. psychotic

    c. socially maladjusted

    d. disruptive

3. During the past decade, the prevalence of students with emotional disturbance has

    a. mostly increased

    b. mostly decreased

    c. remained constant

    d. increased then decreased

4. The wide variation of prevalence for emotional disturbance between states results from

   a. having fewer students with the disability in rural than
      in urban areas

   b. differences in definition and classification practices

   c. some states having lower referral rates for special edu-
      cation services

   d. variation in student behavior from state to state

5. In most states, the prevalence of emotional disturbance is
   related to

   a. gender and age

   b. school discipline policies

   c. general age of parents

   d. intelligence level and social behavior

6. A condition characterized by loss of contact with reality,
   bizarre thought processes, and extremely inappropriate
   behavior is called

   a. social maladjustment

   b. schizophrenia

   c. social problems

   d. temper tantrums

7. Terms used to describe students with emotional disturbance may be similar to those used to describe students
   with learning disabilities and mental retardation, and most
   of the terms are

   a. educational

   b. positive

c. negative

d. psychological

8. Unproductive ways individuals respond in interactions with other people may be called

a. emotional problems

b. social problems

c. psychological problems

d. communication problems

9. Most students with emotional disturbance

a. have physical disabilities

b. have physical and mental disabilities

c. have mental disabilities

d. are physically like their peers

10. The primary area in which students with emotional disturbance are said to differ from their peers is in the area of

a. behavior

b. achievement

c. communication

d. learning

REFLECTION

After you answer the multiple-choice questions, think about how you would answer the following questions:

- What factors might affect the academic success of individuals with emotional disturbance?
- What factors might cause students to exhibit emotional and social problems?
- What do effective teachers do to provide support for students with emotional disturbance?

Answer Key for Self-Assessments

1. b

2. c

3. c

4. b

5. a

6. b

7. c

8. b

9. d

10. a

On Your Own

☑ Make a list of behaviors that might be exhibited by a student with a low self-concept or poor self-esteem.

☑ Make a list of activities you could use to improve the self-concept or self-esteem of your students.

☑ Prepare a table illustrating the numbers of students with specific learning disabilities, communication disorders, mental retardation, and emotional disturbance in your state and a few neighboring states. Compare the figures and come up with three reasons for any variations you identify.

☑ Interview a teacher of students with emotional disturbance. Ask the teacher to describe the emotional and social problems evident in his or her classroom. Ask for recommendations of appropriate instructional methods to use in teaching in an elementary, middle, or high school. Ask the teacher to list reasons that students with emotional disturbance are successful or unsuccessful in school. Ask the teacher to list the special materials used to meet the needs of students from diverse racial and ethnic backgrounds.

☑ Select a journal that focuses on students with emotional disturbance (see Resources). Browse the most recent issues in your library. Note the types of articles that are included (e.g., research, opinion, practical suggestions). Find at least three articles that describe specific teaching activities that you could use to reduce behavior problems. Find at least three articles that describe specific teaching activities that you could use to improve the academic performance of students with emotional disturbance.

☑ To understand how people with emotional problems are treated, try some of these simulations, and note reactions of people around you:

– Wear a heavy coat on a hot summer day.

– Take a ride on public transportation, and talk to yourself during the trip.

☑ Make a list of the rules you would want in your classroom. Describe the plan you would use if students failed to follow the rules.

☑ Interview three professionals who work with people with emotional disturbance in three settings other than school. Ask them to describe what they do and any special methods they use to improve social and emotional problems.

Resources

BOOKS

Adamec, C. (1996). *How to live with a mentally ill person: A handbook of day-to-day strategies*. New York: John Wiley & Sons. (800) 225-5945. *www.wiley.com*.

Algozzine, B. (1997). *Problem behavior management: Educator's resource service*. Gaithersburg, MD: Aspen. This comprehensive publication provides up-to-date teaching tips and information describing a variety of instructional approaches appropriate for students with emotional and social problems.

Allen, C. (1985). *Tea with demons*. New York: Morrow. These recollections of a 30-year-old housewife describing aspects of emotional disturbance comprise an excellent book for high school students.

Axline, V. M. (1964). *Dibs in search of self*. New York: Ballantine Books. A true story about a troubled little boy as told by his therapist, *Dibs* has become a classic in the field of emotional disturbance.

Coleman, M. C., & Webber, J. (2002). *Behavior disorders: Theory and practice* (4th ed.). Englewood Cliffs, NJ: Prentice Hall. This overview of the field of behavior disorders provides information on definitions, characteristics, prevalence, assessment, etiologies, and instructional practices. It is focused heavily on educational programs and concerns.

Craig, E. (1972). *P.S. You're not listening.* New York: New American Library. This is a compilation of teaching success stories.

Erickson, M. T. (1992). *Behavior disorders of children and adolescents: Assessment, etiology, and intervention.* Englewood Cliffs, NJ: Prentice Hall. This text offers a comprehensive discussion of causes, identification, and treatment related to emotional disturbance in children and young adults.

Hayden, T. L. (1988). *Just another kid.* New York: Avon. The book is a teacher's description of one school year in a special education classroom for six students with emotional disturbance.

Heide, F. P. (1976). *Growing anyway up.* New York: Harper. A young girl with emotional disturbance is alienated from her mother and finds it difficult adjusting to a new private school in this excellent book for upper elementary and middle school students.

Jordan, D. (2000). *A guidebook for parents of children with emotional or behavior disorders* (2nd ed.). Minneapolis, MN: Pacer Center. (952) 838-9000 or (952) 838-0190 (TTY). *www.pacer.org.*

Jordan, D. (2000). *Honorable intentions: A parent's guide to educational planning for children with emotional or behavioral disorders* (2nd ed.). Minneapolis, MN: Pacer Center. (952) 838-9000 or (952) 838-0190 (TTY). *www.pacer.org.*

Kauffman, J. M. (1993). *Characteristics of emotional and behavior disorders of children and youth* (5th ed.). New York: Merrill. This text offers a comprehensive overview of the emotional and behavioral characteristics of children and youth with emotional disturbance, including a discussion of historical factors, assessment, and intervention.

Kerr, M. M., & Nelson, C. M. (1989). *Strategies for managing behavior problems in the classroom* (2nd ed.). Columbus, OH: Merrill. Guidelines and strategies are provided for implementing interventions for a variety of common classroom behavior problems.

Koplewicz, H. S. (1996). *It's nobody's fault: New hope and help for difficult children*. New York: Random House/Times Books. (800) 733-3000. *www.randomhouse.com*.

Long, N., Morse, W., & Newman, R. (Eds.). (1980). *Conflict in the classroom: The education of emotionally disturbed children* (4th ed.). Belmont, CA: Wadsworth. This compilation of stories, opinion papers, and articles dealing with various aspects of emotional disturbance, although somewhat dated, is a classic textbook for the introductory course in many teacher preparation programs.

MacCracken, M. (1973). *A circle of children*. New York: New American Library. MacCracken offers a compilation of stories about successful teaching experiences with students with emotional disturbance.

Morgan, D. P., & Jenson, W. R. (1988). *Teaching behaviorally disordered students: Preferred practices*. Columbus, OH: Merrill. This practical methods book provides information on assessment, behavior management, mainstreaming, and teaching academic and social skills.

Rhode, G., Jenson, W. R., & Reavis, H. K. (1992). *The tough kid book: Practical classroom management strategies*. Longmont, CO: Sopris West Educational Services. This resource describes research-validated solutions designed to reduce disruptive classroom behavior.

Rosenberg, M. S., Wilson, R., Maheady, L., & Sindelar, P. T. (1992). *Educating students with behavior disorders*. Boston: Allyn & Bacon. Definitional matters, assessing and classifying disordered behavior, and methods for managing hyperactive, aggressive, socially withdrawn, and rule-breaking behaviors as well as students with severe behavior disorders are discussed.

Snyder, Z. K. (1972). *The witches of worm*. New York: Macmillan. In this excellent book for upper elementary and middle school students, a girl with emotional disturbance believes her selfish and destructive behavior is caused by witches.

Wilen, T. E. (1998). *Straight talk about psychiatric medications for kids*. New York: Guilford. (800) 365-7006. *www.guilford.com*.

JOURNALS AND ARTICLES

American Journal of Orthopsychiatry (AJO). AJO is dedicated to informing public policy, professional practice, and knowledge production related to mental health and human development. Articles related to clinical practice, theory, research, and exposition are among those included. Editor, *American Journal of Orthopsychiatry*, Dept. of Public Policy, George Mason University, 3401 North Fairfax Drive, Arlington, VA 22201–4498.

Behavior Modification (BM). BM is an interdisciplinary journal that publishes research and clinical papers in the area of applied behavior modification. The articles typically contain sufficient detail so readers will understand what was done, how it was done, and why the method of behavior change was selected. Assessment and intervention methods for problems in psychiatric, clinical, educational, and rehabilitation settings are included in most issues. For more information, contact: Michel Hersen, PhD, ABPP, *Behavior Modification*, School of Professional Psychology, Pacific University, 2004 Pacific Avenue, Forest Grove, OR 97116–2328.

Behavior Therapy (BT) is an international journal devoted to the application of behavioral and cognitive sciences to correcting clinical problems. Original research of an experimental or clinical nature which contributes to theory, practice, or evaluation of behavior therapy is primarily what is included in each issue; case studies, clinical replication studies, book reviews, and invited papers are sometimes included. Editor,

David A. F. Haaga, PhD, Department of Psychology, Asbury Building, American University, Washington, DC 20016–8062.

Behavioral Disorders (BD). BD is a publication of the Council for Exceptional Children. Its purpose is to publish research articles of interest to professionals working with students with behavioral disorders. Evaluations of interventions and position papers related to issues of interest to the field are frequently published. Frederick J. Brigham, Curry School of Education, 405 Emmet Street, University of Virginia, Charlottesville, VA 22093.

Beyond Behavior (BB). BB is a publication of the Council for Exceptional Children that provides thought-provoking pieces, fiction, personal stories, and humor papers related to teaching and working with students with behavior disorders. Nancy Meadows, Editor of *Beyond Behavior*, n.meadows@tcu.edu.

Jolivette, K., Barton-Arwood, S., & Scott, T. (2000). Functional behavior assessment as a collaborative process among professionals. *Education and Treatment of Children, 23,* 298–313. The article gives an overview of the principles of functional behavior assessment, illustrating its value as a collaborative practice in special education.

Journal of Abnormal Child Psychology (JACP). JACP is devoted to studies of behavioral pathology in childhood and adolescence. Contents include empirical investigations in etiology, assessment, treatment in community and correctional settings, prognosis and follow-up, epidemiology, remediation in educational settings, pharmacological intervention, and other studies related to abnormal behavior. Susan B. Campbell, Department of Psychology, University of Pittsburgh, 210 South Bouquet Street, MPAC Bldg., 3rd Floor, Pittsburgh, PA 15260.

Journal of Applied Behavior Analysis (JABA). JABA is primarily a publication of reports of experimental research involving applications of the experimental analysis of behavior to solutions of problems of broad social importance. Technical articles relevant to such research and discussions of issues arising from applications are also published. The journal is published quarterly by the Society for the Experimental Analysis of Behavior. Wayne Fisher, Editor, Marcus Institute, 1920 Briarcliff Road, Atlanta, GA 30329.

Journal of Emotional and Behavioral Disorders (JEBD). JEBD is a multidisciplinary publication containing articles on research and practice related to individuals with emotional and behavioral disorders. It includes original research reports, reviews of research, descriptions of practices and effective programs, and discussions of key applied issues that are of interest to a wide range of disciplines. Dr. Michael Epstein, Editor *JEBD*, Department of Educational Psychology, Northern Illinois University, DeKalb, IL 60115–2854 or Dr. Douglas Cullinan, Editor *JEBD*, Department of Curriculum and Instruction, North Carolina State University, Raleigh, NC 27695–7801 or Pro-Ed Publications, 8700 Shoal Creek Blvd., Austin, TX 78757–6897.

Journal of the Experimental Analysis of Behavior (JEAB). JEAB is published bimonthly by the Society for the Experimental Analysis of Behavior. *JEAB* is primarily for the original publication of experiments relevant to the behavior of individual organisms. Review articles and theoretical papers also appear. Kennon A. Lattal, Department of Psychology, West Virginia University, Morgantown, West Virginia 26506–6040.

Nelson, J.R., Crabtree, M., Marchard-Martella, N., & Martella, R. (1998). Teaching good behavior in the whole school. *Teaching Exceptional Children, 30*(4), 4–9. Information about using school-wide interventions to improve behavior problems is offered.

Scott, T. M. (2002). Removing roadblocks to effective behavior intervention in inclusive settings: Responding to typical objections by school personnel. *Beyond Behavior, 12,* 21–26. The article offers a brief overview of empirically derived behavior interventions and an exploration of arguments used by school personnel to avoid using them.

The Behavior Analyst (TBA). TBA is published by the Society for the Advancement of Behavior Analysis. Articles in *TBA* are informative about various aspects of instruction and training in behavior analysis that are of use to the public as well as professionals concerned with improving behavior. Carol Pilgrim, Department of Psychology, University of North Carolina–Wilmington, 601 S. College Road, Wilmington, NC 28403–3297.

ORGANIZATIONS

American Academy of Child and Adolescent Psychiatry

The American Academy of Child and Adolescent Psychiatry is a professional medical organization made up of child and adolescent psychiatrists and is aimed at continuing education, collaboration, and training for the members. Public Information Office, 3615 Wisconsin Ave. NW, Washington, DC 20016. (202) 966-7300. *www.aacap.org.*

American Orthopsychiatric Association (AOA)

AOA brings together professionals in all disciplines devoted to mental health and human development. Members apply a multidisciplinary approach to address issues affecting families, children, adolescents, adults, and school and community mental health. AOA members are innovators and are less likely to accept the status quo or to work within the confines of a single discipline. AOA provides annual meetings and professional publications. AOA, 19 West 44th Street, Suite 1616, New York, NY 10036.

Association for Behavior Analysis (ABA)

ABA advances the science of behavior analysis and its application. The purview of ABA encompasses contemporary scientific and social issues, theoretical advances, and the dissemination of professional and public information about behavior analysis and behavior change. ABA activities include membership services, journal support, directories, *ABA Newsletter,* and an annual convention. Susan Goeters, ABA, 258 Wood Hall, Western Michigan University, Kalamazoo, MI 49008.

Council for Children With Behavioral Disorders (CCBD)

A division of the Council for Exceptional Children (CEC), CCBD pursues quality educational services and program alternatives for children and youth with behavioral disorders, advocates for their needs, and emphasizes research and professional growth. The approximately 8,600 members include teachers, parents, and mental health professionals. Members receive *Behavioral Disorders, Beyond Behavior,* and the *CCBD Newsletter.* CEC, 1100 North Glebe Road, Suite 300, Arlington, VA 22201–5704.

Federation of Families for Children's Mental Health

This is a family-run organization that, through its nationwide network, helps children with mental health needs and their families to improve their quality of life. 1101 King Street, Suite 420, Alexandria, VA 22314. (703) 684-7710; ffcmh@ffcmh.org. *www.ffcmh.org.*

National Alliance for the Mentally Ill (NAMI)

Founded in 1979, NAMI supports those living with mental illnesses through education, research, and advocacy. NAMI, Colonial Place Three, 2107 Wilson Boulevard, Suite 300, Arlington, VA 22203–3754. (703) 524-7600; (703) 516-7227 (TTY); (800) 950-6264; namiofc@aol.com. *www.nami.org.*

National Information Center for Children and Youth With Disabilities (NICHCY)

NICHCY is the national information center that provides information on disabilities and disability-related issues. It has many publications in English and Spanish. NICHCY, P.O. Box 1492, Washington, DC 20013; (800) 695-0285 (Voice/TTY); nichcy@aed.org; *www.nichcy.org.*

National Mental Health Association (NMHA)

Established in 1907, NMHA encourages reform in the treatment of those with mental health disabilities. NMHA, 1021 Prince Street, Alexandria, VA 22314–2971. (703) 684-7722; (800) 969-6642; (800) 433-5959 (TTY); nmhainfo@aol.com. *www .nmha.org.*

Society for the Advancement of Behavior Analysis (SABA)

SABA provides instruction and training in behavior analysis and disseminates information. Its members also offer research and practical applications of behavior analysis to solve community, educational, and social problems. Susan Goeters, SABA, 258 Wood Hall, Western Michigan University, Kalamazoo, MI 49008.

Society for the Experimental Analysis of Behavior (SEAB)

SEAB is concerned with research and the practical applications of behavior analysis. SEAB exists primarily for the purpose of overseeing the publication of the *Journal of the Experimental Analysis of Behavior (JEAB)* and the *Journal of Applied Behavior Analysis (JABA).* The organization does not hold annual meetings, but does participate in and subsidize panels and symposia at the annual meetings of the Association for Behavior Analysis. Devonia Stein, SEAB, Department of Psychology, Indiana University, Bloomington, IN 47405.

References

Anderegg, M. L., Baker, J., Brewster, L., Cohn, J., Deanda, L., Donovan, M., Gaudes, Y., Gruenhagen, K., & Riddle, G. (1993). Top thirty. *Beyond Behavior, 5*(1), 24–25.

Coleman, M. C., & Webber, J. (2002). *Behavior disorders: Theory and practice* (4th ed.). Boston: Allyn & Bacon.

Council for Children With Behavioral Disorders (CCBD): Executive Committee. (1987). Position paper on definition and identification of students with behavioral disorders. *Behavioral Disorders, 13*, 9–19.

Individuals With Disabilities Education Act, 34 C.F.R. § 300.7 (1997).

National Dissemination Center for Children With Disabilities. (2004, January). *Emotional Disturbance* (Fact Sheet 5). Washington, DC: Author. Retrieved December 30, 2005, from http://www.nichcy.org/pubs/factshe/fs5txt.htm.

Rose, L. C., & Gallup, A. M. (2002). Thirty-fourth annual Phi Delta Kappa/Gallup poll of the public's attitudes toward the public schools. *Phi Delta Kappa, 84,* 41–46, 51–56.

Rose, L. C., & Gallup, A. M. (2003). Thirty-fifth annual Phi Delta Kappa/Gallup poll of the public's attitudes toward the public schools. *Phi Delta Kappa, 84,* 41–46, 51–56.

Rose, L. C., & Gallup, A. M. (2004). Thirty-sixth annual Phi Delta Kappa/Gallup poll of the public's attitudes toward the public schools. *Phi Delta Kappa, 84,* 41–46, 51–56.

U.S. Department of Education. (2000). *Twenty-second annual report to Congress on the implementation of the Individuals With Disabilities Education Act.* Washington, DC: Author.

U.S. Department of Education. (2001). *Twenty-third annual report to Congress on the implementation of the Individuals With Disabilities Education Act.* Washington, DC: Author.

U.S. Department of Education. (2002). *Twenty-fourth annual report to Congress on the implementation of the Individuals With Disabilities Education Act.* Washington, DC: Author.

Index

Note: Numbers in **Bold** followed by a colon [:] denote the book number within which the page numbers are found.

**CORWIN
PRESS**

The Corwin Press logo—a raven striding across an open book—represents the union of courage and learning. Corwin Press is committed to improving education for all learners by publishing books and other professional development resources for those serving the field of PreK–12 education. By providing practical, hands-on materials, Corwin Press continues to carry out the promise of its motto: **"Helping Educators Do Their Work Better."**